Michael Morpurgo

PRIVATE PEACEFUL

adapted by Simon Reade

OBERON BOOKS
LONDON

WWW.OBERONBOOKS.COM

First published in 2006 by Oberon Books Ltd
521 Caledonian Road, London N7 9RH
Tel: +44 (0) 20 7607 3637 / Fax: +44 (0) 20 7607 3629
e-mail: info@oberonbooks.com
www.oberonbooks.com

Reprinted in this single edition in 2012

A catalogue record for this book is available from the British Library.

PB ISBN: 978-1-84943-501-7
Digital ISBN: 978-1-84943-571-0

Cover image by Matt Humphrey from the feature film *Private
Peaceful*, a Fluidity Films production.

Printed, bound and converted
by CPI Group (UK) Ltd, Croydon, CR0 4YY.

Visit www.oberonbooks.com to read more about all our books
and to buy them. You will also find features, author interviews and
news of any author events, and you can sign up for e-newsletters
so that you're always first to hear about our new releases.

Contents

Finding Private Peaceful

by Michael Morpurgo

I was born in 1943, near London. I played in bomb sites, listened to the stories told around the kitchen table, stories of war that saddened all the faces around me. My Uncle Pieter lived only in the photo on the mantelpiece. He had been killed in the RAF in 1941. But for me he lived on, ever young in the photograph, as I grew up, as I grew old.

So I have been drawn instinctively, I think, in many of my stories, to the subject of war, the enduring of it, the pity of it, and above all the suffering of survivors. Some thirty years ago, after meeting an old soldier from my village who had been to the First World War in the Devon Yeomanry in the Cavalry, I wrote *War Horse*, a vision of that dreadful war seen through the eyes of a horse.

Then, almost ten years ago, on a visit to Ypres to talk about writing about war for young people at a conference, I visited the In Flanders Fields Museum.

Talking to Piet Chielens, its director, I was reminded that over 300 British soldiers had been executed during the First World War for cowardice or desertion, two of them for simply falling asleep at their posts.

I read their stories, their trials (some lasted less than twenty minutes – twenty minutes for a man's life). They knew then about shell shock – many officers were treated in psychiatric hospitals for it, Wilfred Owen and Siegfried Sassoon amongst them. They knew even as they sentenced these men (they called them 'worthless' men), that most of them were traumatized by the terrors they had endured, by the prolonged and dreadful brutality of trench warfare.

In all, over 3,000 were condemned to death, and 300 of them were chosen to be shot. I visited the execution sites, the cells in Poperinghe, I read the telegram sent home to a mother informing her that her son had been shot at dawn for cowardice. I knew recent governments had considered and rejected the granting of pardons for these men, had refused to acknowledge the appalling injustice visited upon them.

Standing in a war cemetery in the rain five miles outside Ypres, I came upon the gravestone of Private Peaceful. I had found my name, my Unknown Soldier. I had found my story, a story I knew I had to tell and that should be told.

The question then was how it should be told. I decided to put myself at the centre of the story, to become the condemned man waiting only for dawn and death. A glance at my watch, recently returned from the menders who had declared it was made in 1915, gave me the idea that the chapter breaks should happen only when the soldier glances down at his watch which he dreads to do, and tries not to do.

My soldier would reflect on his life, live it again through the night so that the night would be long, as long as his life. He does not want to sleep his last night away, nor waste it in dreams. Above all he wants to feel alive.

Each chapter begins in the barn in Belgium, but his thoughts soon take him back to Devon, to the fields and streams and lanes of Iddesleigh, his home and his village.

Memories of his childhood come back to him, of family. Of the first day at school, of the first stirrings of love, a father's death, a night's poaching; then of the first news of approaching war and the recruiting sergeant in the town square at Hatherleigh. So to the trenches and to the events that have led him to the last night of his life.

And all the while the watch he does not want to look at is ticking his life away.

In the First World War, between 1914 and 1918, over 290 soldiers of the British and Commonwealth armies were executed by firing squad, some for desertion, some for cowardice, two for simply sleeping at their posts.

Many of these men were traumatized by shell shock. Courts martial were brief, the accused often unrepresented.

The injustice they suffered at the start of the 20th century was only officially recognised by the British Government at the beginning of the 21st century and some ninety years later the men were granted posthumous pardons.

Staging Private Peaceful

by Mark Leipacher

Private Peaceful has been on a long journey, not just from the fields of Devon to the battlefields of Ypres. The enduring, global appetite for the production lies in the universal appeal of Michael Morpurgo's rite-of-passage tale, and the theatricality of Simon Reade's adaptation. A lone actor stands on a stage and conjures the many different characters, their various moods and emotional states and – with the support of brilliantly designed lighting and sound – the multitude of environments they inhabit.

There's very little on stage with the actor. He's wearing his costume – or uniform. There's a bed, which anchors us back in the barn but is upstage enough to fade away when Tommo begins creating and colouring the history of his life. Handily, this sweeps to centre stage to become a bunker and, with its exposed bed springs, the barbed wire of a trench overlooking no-man's-land.

Like Simon's dramaturgical paring down of the script, the other paraphernalia – mud rows, barbed wire – are usually discarded and even props, like a mess tin, have been eliminated during different mountings of the production. There are two obvious essential exceptions: Molly's letter and the watch with which Tommo measures out his final hours.

Staging *Private Peaceful* is very much focused on the actor and the words. A subtle change in physicality, a modulation of the voice, a variation in focus and eyeline, a change in tempo and speech patterns, the inner emotional core, the actor uses a range of techniques to bring each character vividly to life.

Five actors have now played Tommo, and the strength of the material – the recurring motifs of birds, numbers, hands, the earth – provide an essential framework within which each actor has used his own imaginative approach. In their different interpretations, the Sergeant Major in the town square has been a preening cockerel, Sergeant Hanley a savage Dobermann, and the Old Lady has run the entire spectrum from hilarious dame to terrifying crone.

Imagination is the crucial component. Theatre of this kind is a conjuring trick, a sleight of hand that not only the actor but also the audience must completely buy into. In the storytelling, Tommo explains to us where he is and what he is acting out. For the most part – though there are exceptions – it's crucial that the actor completes the activity on the word and through the line. If he describes something and then acts it out, or completes an activity and then tells us what he's done, there's a peculiar disconnection and the fragile fabric of the illusion – the make-believe – that's being created can start to disintegrate, like a YouTube video when the images and the sound start sliding out of sync. It's vital that the audience are given all of the conditions to use their imaginations and that they share the understanding of the story with the actor.

Private Peaceful is a play that transcends demographic make-up and cultural background. The actor and the audience experience the joy and innocence of childhood and the horror and realities of war. As Simon says, 'it's for anyone with an imagination.'

Private Peaceful – Timeline

1898	Thomas Peaceful born
1901	Queen Victoria dies
1908	Tommo starts school
1914	Tommo leaves school **28 June**: Archduke Ferdinand assassinated in Sarajevo **August**: War declared **Autumn**: Tommo arrives at the Western Front
1915	**22 April – 25 May**: Second Battle of Ypres – the Germans deploy chlorine gas for the first time **Summer**: Little Tommo born
1916	**25 June, 6am**: Firing Squad **1 July – 18 November**: Battle of the Somme
1917	**Spring**: America enters the War
1918	**11 November**: The War ends

The Last Laugh

'O Jesus Christ! I'm hit,' he said; and died.
Whether he vainly cursed, or prayed indeed,
The Bullets chirped – In vain! vain! vain!
Machine-guns chuckled, – Tut-tut! Tut-tut!
And the Big Gun guffawed.

Another sighed, – 'O Mother, mother! Dad!'
Then smiled, at nothing, childlike, being dead.
And the lofty Shrapnel-cloud
Leisurely gestured, – Fool!
And the falling splinters tittered.

'My love!' one moaned. Love-languid seemed his mood,
Til, slowly lowered, his whole face kissed the mud.
And the Bayonets' long teeth grinned;
Rabbles of Shells hooted and groaned;
And the Gas hissed.

Wilfred Owen, February 1918

Adapting Private Peaceful

an Interview with the adaptor & director, Simon Reade,
by Gill Foreman

Q. How did the *Private Peaceful* journey begin for you?

SR: I was lying in the bath one morning. The BBC's arts correspondent, Rebecca Jones, was on Radio 4's *Today* programme interviewing the then Children's Laureate, Michael Morpurgo, about his forthcoming book, *Private Peaceful*. Michael talked about some First World War soldiers, these young boys who signed up underage, often with the collusion of the people who signed them up. They went to the Front, got shell shock and some were tried and sentenced to be shot at dawn for cowardice in the face of the enemy, or desertion or insubordination. We now realise that this was technically illegal, even according to army rules then, but they had still not been granted a pardon in Britain when Michael's book was published in 2003. France had granted posthumous pardons, as had New Zealand. Our government had always refused.

Michael Morpurgo was talking about the book from this political perspective, but then he began to read from it, and as he read, I thought, 'This is amazing! This is a dramatic monologue, all from the point of view of this young soldier'. Unusually for First World War literature, it's from the point of view of a private rather than an officer. We think of Siegfried Sassoon, Wilfred Owen – even Sebastian Faulks' *Birdsong* – their writing is from the point of view of the Officer class; and *Private Peaceful* is from the point of view of a very simple person, and not even an urban person but a rural one.

Q. What was your process in adapting the novel?
Did all the material come from the novel or did you
change things?

SR: When you take a novel and put it into the theatre, you have to make it work as a piece of theatre. So, of course, you are faithful to the original spirit of a work, but the first thing that you look for are all the dramatic arcs and journeys and when there are hurdles to jump. *Private Peaceful* is a rite-of-passage story with lots of dramatic vignettes along the way. It is about a young boy growing up; it's also about the little man fighting against, or fighting within, something that the state and the world order is imposing upon him.

The changes that you make in adapting are that you take out anything that doesn't serve the essential dramatic purpose. The most important aspect that people will notice I have changed in this adaptation is the ending. What Michael does very cleverly in the novel is to pull off a great literary conceit. [SPOILER ALERT] All the way through you think it's Tommo who is going to die, but of course it is Tommo's brother, Charlie, and it's only right at the end that there's this twist. In the theatre, my first instinct in adapting the novel was that this ending might prove disappointing in the sense that we will have lived with this one person, Tommo, all the way through the evening – one actor playing all the parts – and in the end he should pay the ultimate sacrifice to complete the most extreme dramatic journey. So I decided to kill him. [END OF SPOILER ALERT] Michael recognised that this would work in the theatre, especially in the context of a one-man show, and wouldn't harm his novel, because his novel is always there for people to read. What I was naïve about at the time, perhaps, was just how widely read Michael's novel would be so that many, if not most, people seeing the play for the first time will have already read the novel and appreciate its ins and outs intimately. However, I stand by the ending I have created for the one-man show, because, although it is brutal, it does make total theatrical and dramatic sense. I have also had the good fortune to adapt the story for a young cast of thirty, and for the radio, and for the cinema, and in each of those adaptations it has made more dramatic sense to restore Michael's original ending.

Q. What made you choose to make it a one-man show?
SR: The material demanded it. Everything is seen from Tommo's perspective and you don't get other people's perspective, really Tommo conjures all this up in these last hours of his life. I think that the most faithful way of adapting this for the stage is to do it as a one-man show where he creates everything before his and the audience's very eyes. And it's also a pragmatic choice, of course, in terms of economies of scale. But that has been to

the benefit of audiences because it has meant that the original production has been revived time and time again.

Q. How does *Private Peaceful* relate to a young audience as a piece of theatre?
SR: First of all, it speaks directly to the experiences of somebody who has gone from pre-pubescence, to pubescence, through adolescence and into young adulthood. That obviously speaks to young people.

Secondly, the reason that the First World War has always resonated with young people is that a lot of young people were the cannon fodder, dying for a cause that they really didn't understand – and if they did, they may well have deplored once they had endured the fighting. So, *Private Peaceful* touches all sorts of political and emotional buttons in young people. Connected with that of course, is that the story is retold in the context of the latest wars in Iraq, Afghanistan, Syria, Libya – Africa – where young people, as young as teenagers, die for the political ends of America, the African warlords, Britain and the rest of the European Allies, Assad. There's an immediate connection with young men, and now women, going off to war. You can take a classic war and superimpose it on the present, without being too crass about it.

Thirdly, this is the kind of play-acting that you can imagine somebody doing in their own bedroom: tipping their bed over and saying, 'now this is a trench', or being one moment at home and the next in the middle of a market square, simply by articulating it. It's non-literal theatre and children have the imagination to make that leap. And for adults watching it, it reawakens our childlike imagination; it has a young spirit about it.

Q. What do you think that the theatre performance gives to the audience that they don't get by reading the book?
SR: There's a magical alchemy in theatre where you get excited by the artifice of it. You get transported on extraordinary journeys of the imagination with very few tricks, by the power of the word. There's something brilliant about the imagination and the transformation that happens in theatre when you have to engage with it actively. And not as one reader but as a group of people bearing witness.

Q. What does a good piece of dramatic writing contain?
SR: When you look for a good story, you look for a journey in which you have been transformed as an actor or as a member of the audience, or where the story has completely transformed all the characters in it. If you do something that is just a slice of life, it can get really dreary, in my view. Incidentally, that's why the really good soaps – well-written like episodes of *EastEnders*, *Casualty*, *The Archers* – are at their best when they are fantastically operatic rather than humdrum, banal.

I always ask of a story, 'Has this got drama?' But what does this mean? It means that you have a protagonist and an antagonist and they've got a hurdle to jump over. One of them will win and one of them will lose, and then you'll get into another situation and that will synthesise and will form the next step of the drama. Aristotelian. Dialectic. Call it what you will; it's swings-and-roundabouts dramatic.

Q. Did you make lots of changes to the *Private Peaceful* script in the original rehearsals?
SR: Yes. Most of the changes that we made were cuts. I'm a great believer in cutting. When I was the dramaturg at the RSC I never talked about the text, I always talked about the script because scripts are great malleable things that exist to be chopped and changed and recreated time and time again by actors, directors, designers and the rest of the creative team. They're not authoritative texts, not sacrosanct blueprints; they're actually raw material. With all those new plays pouring out of the Elizabethan theatre's star writers, I imagine they would turn up at rehearsals with their scripts and cut and alter and adapt as they went along because they'd recognize the collaborative nature of creating work in the theatre. And you respond to actors creating roles. Shakespeare might have said: 'I really fancy the talents of the boy playing Juliet; I'm going to give him/her a good speech in Act 4.' Or: 'Wow! Yet again my lead actor playing Mercutio is fantastic; let's rewrite something for him now'.

When you approach theatrical literature it's rough and it's ready and you suit the particular nuances of the actor that you've got, of the time that you are living in. This play was an adaptation of Michael's original story, recreated for the theatre, with my own writer's vision of it, made afresh by me as director and by Paul

Chequer as performer, the actor who played the part originally – Paul created the role, like a prima ballerina creates her role that is then recreated, reinterpreted by subsequent ballerinas, just as four subsequent actors have recreated and reinvented the role of Tommo for themselves in this production.

Q. How did you work in rehearsals?

SR: We did a lot of character work in rehearsal, looked at the detail. Obviously the main part is Tommo, but what we didn't want to do was to make all the other characters caricatures. We wanted them to seem rounded. Even though we may only meet people very briefly, we want the audience to feel like they know them. In the book, Michael sets things up that you think are quite innocuous at the beginning; for example, Jimmy Parsons has the fight with Charlie and gets smacked in the goolies – it's a snigger line of course: goolies. But it's more than that: procreation; manhood. And then it's Jimmy Parsons who actually is the most cowardly person. But he's the first person to volunteer as well. You learn a lot about Jimmy Parsons even though you're hardly ever introduced to him at all. You just associate him with that one fun word – goolies.

Q. Can theatre be a catalyst for change, political or otherwise?

SR: Yes, I think so; not necessarily on its own, although there will be examples of that. It can be part of a cumulative effect. I do believe you can become a more joyful, rounded person if you appreciate poetry and you see great theatre and enjoy films – and watch good football matches. I think theatre is part and parcel of our rich culture. I think it would be naïve to say any one particular play can have that effect alone.

We've played *Private Peaceful* to lots of adults – adults coming to the theatre unaccompanied by children. Adults are very moved by the play in a way that they might not have expected to be. When we think back to when we were, say, twelve, we were idealistic. Good theatre can make you tap into the idealism you had before we all became pragmatic and compromised and adult and dreary.

Q. Why do you think that it took so long for these soldiers to be granted a posthumous pardon?

SR: Michael threw down the gauntlet when the book was published in 2003 by saying that it is surely a mark of a civilized people to admit its wrongdoings of the past. When we came to produce the play for the first time in 2004, that challenge had yet to be picked up, which made me conclude that so-called Great Britain wasn't really a cradle of civilization after all. Some people made those overfamiliar, jaded, specious arguments about not judging the past by today's values – in fact Michael Portillo said words to that effect in a review of our production in Edinburgh in the *New Statesman* for whom he was theatre critic at the time; he was otherwise impressed with the show, but it didn't move him to feel remorse for not using his powers when he was Defence Secretary to grant the pardons. It took a few more years – and a few more thousand book sales and performances of *Private Peaceful*, at the Trafalgar Studios in Whitehall in particular, and having the *Daily Mail* critic, of all people, championing the cause of posthumous pardons for these dead soldiers – to civilize Great Britain. I'm not saying Michael's book, or our play, was single-handedly responsible. But I like to think that we played a modest part in the accumulation of self-evident truth that led to the British government eventually atoning for the sins of the State.

We often think we can't change things; we make excuses about having to do things by stealth, 'softly softly catchee monkey', by making evolutionary progress. We don't want to upset the apple cart. But we should. And if theatre can be part of a constant changing process, a social revolution for idealistic young people to tip those carts over then we can all scrump those apples for the greater good…although perhaps I shouldn't over-extend the metaphor. Or sound off about politics. I'm a theatre-maker, a dramatist. Let the play speak for itself.

PRIVATE PEACEFUL

Characters

TOMMO

Note

The actor playing Tommo delivers all the lines in the play. Other characters' speech is indicated thus:

(CHARACTER NAME.)

The style of the production is to tell the story as simply as possible, with the set and props pared down to the military clothes the performer stands up in, and the bed Tommo lies in – which is turned on its side for the trench, for example. The rest of Tommo's world is created by engaging the audience's imagination.

Private Peaceful was first performed on 7 April 2004 at Bristol Old Vic's Studio theatre, with the following company:

TOMMO, Paul Chequer

Director, Simon Reade
Designer, Bill Talbot
Lighting Designer, Tim Streader
Sound Designer, Jason Barnes
Stage Manager, Juliette Taylor
Production Manager, Jo Cuthbert
Studio Technician, Olly Hellis
Casting Advisor, Amy Ball
Dialect, Charmian Hoare

The production has subsequently toured throughout the UK and played in Ireland, Off-Broadway, Hong Kong and Wellington, New Zealand, with Tommo played by Alexander Campbell, Finn Hanlon, Mark Quartley and Leon Williams.

The production was revived in September 2012 by Scamp Theatre in association with Poonamallee Productions at the Haymarket Theatre, West End, presented by the National Theatre with the following company:

TOMMO, Paul Chequer / Mark Quartley

Director, Simon Reade
Designer, Bill Talbot
Lighting Designer, Wayne Dowdeswell
Sound Designer, Jason Barnes
Associate Director, Mark Leipacher
Additional Music, Coope, Boyes & Simpson
Stage Manager, Maddy Grant
Production Manager, Bettina Patel

Thanks to Michael and Clare Morpurgo, Alison Reid, Rose and Amy Reade, David Farr, Guy de Beaujeu, Ginny Schiller, Marc Berlin, Anna Schmitz, Robin Hawkes.

Private Peaceful

Ypres. 1916. No-man's-land.
24ᵗʰ June. A barn, a prison. A bed. A bully tin of stew, potatoes.
A pair of boots.

1

(*Private Peaceful – TOMMO, nearly 18 – looks at his watch.*)

BARN

Five past ten.

I have the whole night ahead of me. I shan't sleep. I won't dream it away.

I want to remember everything, just as it was, just as it happened. I've had nearly eighteen years of yesterdays and tomorrows, and tonight I must remember as many of them as I can.

Tonight, more than any other night of my life, I want to feel alive!

ON THE WAY TO SCHOOL

Charlie's leading me by the hand because he knows I don't want to go (to school). I've never worn a collar before and it's choking me. My boots are strange and heavy on my feet. My heart's heavy too. I'm dreading it.

Big Joe doesn't have to go and I don't think that's fair at all. He's much older than me, even a bit older than Charlie. But Big Joe stays at home with Mother, and sits up in his tree singing 'Oranges and Lemons'. He's always laughing. I wish I could be happy like him. I wish I could be at home like him. I don't want to go with Charlie. I DON'T WANT TO GO TO SCHOOL.

Charlie sees my eyes full of tears and knows how it is. He's three years older than me, so he's done everything, knows everything.

(CHARLIE.) Do you want a piggyback, Tommo?

I hop up and cling on tight round Charlie's neck, trying not to whimper.

(CHARLIE.) First day's the worst, Tommo. It's not so bad. Honest.

Whenever Charlie says 'honest', I know it's not true.

(*Sound: bell.*)

OUTSIDE SCHOOL

We line up in two silent rows, about twenty children in each. I recognize some of them from Sunday school. Charlie's no longer beside me. He's in the other line, and he's winking at me. I blink back. I can't wink with one eye. Charlie laughs.

(MR MUNNINGS.) Fall into line!

Mr Munnings: he of the raging temper Charlie's told me so much about. Mr Munnings is pointing right at me and all the other children have turned to look.

(MR MUNNINGS.) Ah! A new boy. A new boy to add to my trials and tribulations. Name, boy?

(TOMMO.) Tommo, sir. Thomas Peaceful.

(MR MUNNINGS.) First a Charlie Peaceful, and now a Thomas Peaceful. Was not one Peaceful enough? Understand this, Thomas Peaceful, that here I am your lord and master. You do what I say when I say it. You do not cheat, you do not lie, you do not blaspheme. These are my commandments. Do I make myself clear?

(TOMMO.) Yes, sir.

Charlie and the big'uns follow Mr Munnings into one classroom. And then I'm taken with the tiddlers into Miss McAllister's.

CLASSROOM

(MISS MCALLISTER.) Thomas, you will be sitting here –

– Miss McAllister is very proper –

(MISS MCALLISTER.) – sitting there, next to Molly. And your bootlaces are undone. Tie them up before you trip.

(TOMMO.) I can't, miss.

(MISS MCALLISTER.) 'Can't' is not a word we use in my class, Thomas Peaceful. We shall just have to teach you how to tie your bootlaces. That's what we're all here for, Thomas: to learn. You show him, Molly. Molly's the oldest girl in my class, Thomas. She'll help you.

Molly doesn't look up at me while she's tying them – but I wish she would. She has chestnut-brown hair the same colour as Father's old horse – and shining – and I want to reach out and touch it. Then at last she looks up at me. I have a friend.

(*Sound: schoolyard; kids playing.*)

SCHOOLYARD

In playtime, in the schoolyard, I want to go over and talk to Molly, but I can't because she's surrounded by a gaggle of giggling girls. They keep looking over their shoulders and laughing at me. I look for Charlie, but he's playing conkers with the big'uns. So I decide to undo my bootlaces and try doing them up again like Molly. I try again and again. It's untidy, it's loose – but I can do it! From across the schoolyard Molly sees, and smiles.

At home I never wear boots, except for church. Father always wore his great hobnail boots, the boots he died in.

IN THE WOODS

In the woods, Father was chopping away at a tree nearby, grunting and groaning at every stroke. At first I think he's just groaning a bit louder. But then the sound seems to be coming from somewhere high up in the branches.

I look up: the great tree is swaying and creaking when all the other trees are standing still, silent. I stand and stare.

(*Sound: tree falling like a roar of thunder.*)

(FATHER.) Run, Tommo! Run!

(*Silence. The tree has fallen.*)

When I came to, I see him at once, see the soles of his boots with their worn nails. One arm is outstretched towards me, his finger points at me. His eyes are open, but I know they're not seeing me. He's not breathing. When I shout at him, when I shake him, he doesn't wake up.

(*Sound: solemn harmonium hymn.*)

CHURCH

In the church we're sat side by side at the front, Mother, Big Joe, Charlie and me. We've never in our lives sat in the front row before. It's where the Colonel always sits. The coffin rests on trestles, Father inside in his Sunday suit. A swallow swoops over our heads all through the prayers and the hymns, flitting from window to window, to belfry, to altar, looking for a way out. And I know for certain it is Father trying to escape. I know because he told us more than once that in his next life he'd like to be a bird, so he could fly free wherever he wanted.

The Colonel gets up into the pulpit:

(COLONEL. *Thumb tucked behind jacket lapel.*) James Peaceful was a good man, one of the best workers I have known, the salt of the earth, always cheerful as he went about his work. The Peaceful family has been employed by my family for five generations. In all his thirty years as a forester on my estate James Peaceful was a credit to his family and village.

While the Colonel's droning on I'm thinking of all the rude things Father used to say about him –

(FATHER.) – silly old fart, mad old duffer –

– and how Mother always said that –

(MOTHER.) – he might well be a 'silly old fart', but it's the Colonel who pays the wages and owns the roof over our heads, so you all show him respect.

GRAVEYARD

The earth thumps down on the coffin (behind us) as we leave the graveside. He was trying to save me. If only I had run, he wouldn't now be lying dead.

All I've ever thought is that I killed my own father.

2

(*TOMMO looks at his watch.*)

BARN

Twenty to eleven.

(*He spoons his food unenthusiastically.*)

I don't want to eat. Stew, potatoes. I usually like stew, but I've no appetite. Not now.

Big Joe ate more than all the rest of us put together – potato pie, cheese and pickle, stew and dumplings, bread and butter pudding – whatever Mother cooked, he'd stuff it in and scoff it down. Anything Charlie and I didn't like we'd shuffle onto his plate when Mother wasn't looking.

Mother told us when we were older that Big Joe nearly died just after he was born. 'Meningitis', the doctor told her at the hospital, 'brain damage'.

She was told 'he wouldn't live or even if he did, he'd be of no use to anyone.'

It was Big Joe who got me into my first fight.

(*Sound: schoolyard; kids playing.*)

SCHOOLYARD

It was playtime. Big Joe had come up to school to see Charlie and me. He stood and watched us from outside the gate, bright-eyed with excitement. I ran over to him. He opened his cupped hands just enough for me to see a slow-worm curled inside.

(TOMMO.) That's lovely, Joe.

Then Big Joe wandered off, walking down the lane, humming:

(BIG JOE. *Humming.*) Oranges and Lemons (*Etc.*)

Someone taps me hard on my shoulder.

(JIMMY PARSONS. *Sneering.*) Who's got a loony for a brother?

(TOMMO.) What did you say, Jimmy Parsons?

(JIMMY PARSONS. *Chanting.*) Your-brother's-a-loony, your-brother's-a-loony.

So I go for him, fists flailing, screaming – but I don't land a single punch. Then Jimmy Parsons hits me full in the face and sends me sprawling. He puts the boot in, kicking and kicking –

– then, suddenly, he stops.

I look up. Charlie's grabbing him round the neck and pulling him to the ground. They're rolling over and over, punching each other and blaspheming. The whole school has gathered round to watch now, shouting and egging them on. 'Go on, Charlie!'

That's when Mr Munnings comes running out, roaring.

(MR MUNNINGS.) What the blazes!

He pulls them apart and drags them off inside the school.

Luckily for me, Mr Munnings never even notices me, bleeding.

They both get the cane, six strokes each.

Molly comes over, takes me by the hand and leads me towards the pump. She soaks her handkerchief under it and dabs my nose and my hands and my knee – the blood is everywhere. The water is cold and soothing, and her hands are soft.

(MOLLY.) I like Big Joe. He's kind. I like people who are kind.

Molly likes Big Joe! It was then that I knew I would love her till the day I die.

Then Charlie comes out into the schoolyard hitching up his trousers and grinning in the sunshine.

(CHARLIE.) Jimmy won't do it again, Tommo. I hit him where it hurts. In the goolies.

We all laughed at that.

(CHARLIE.) Are you all right, Tommo?

(TOMMO.) My nose hurts a bit, Charlie.

(CHARLIE.) Well, so does my bum.

COUNTRYSIDE

Back home we were getting very hungry, without Father. We tried to make ends meet, but all we ever seemed to have for supper were potatoes.

So Charlie had the idea to go poaching. By now, we were best friends with Molly, so she came too. At dusk, or dawn, we'd go off across the Colonel's land, into his forests, fishing in his river. Molly and I would be on look-out while Charlie did the trapping or netting.

We did well. We caught loads of rabbits, a few trout and, once, a fourteen-pound salmon. So now we had something to eat with our potatoes.

MEADOWS

Both of them being older than me – Molly by two years, Charlie by three – they always ran faster than I did, racing ahead of me, leaping the high meadow grass, Molly's plaits whirling about her head, their laughter mingling. When they got too far ahead I sometimes felt they wanted to be without me. But I'd whine and they'd soon wait for me to catch up. Best of all Molly would (sometimes) come running back and take my hand.

BROOK

We'd hare down the hill to the brook, pull off our heavy boots and release our aching feet. We'd sit there on the bank wiggling our toes in the cool water. Then we'd follow the brook home, feet squelching in the mud, our toes oozing with it. I used to love mud, the smell of it, the feel of it, the larking about in it.

RIVERSIDE / POOL

Sometimes we'd go swimming in the river's pool, hung all around by willows, where the water was dark and deep and mysterious, and where no one ever came.

One time, Molly dared Charlie to take off all his clothes – and to my amazement, he did! Then she did!! – and they both ran shrieking and bare-bottomed into the water. When they called me in after them, I wouldn't do it, not in front of Molly. So I sat and sulked on the bank and watched them splashing and giggling, wishing I was with them. Eventually, they persuaded me. Molly stood waist-deep in the river and put her hands over her eyes.

(MOLLY.) Come on, Tommo! I won't watch. Promise.

I stripped off and made a dash for the river, covering myself as I went just in case Molly was peeping through her fingers.

Afterwards, Molly got dressed behind a bush and told us 'not to watch'. But we did. That was the first time I ever saw a girl with no clothes on. She was very thin and white, and she wrung her plaits out like a wet cloth.

Molly told us she wanted to die right there and then, which I thought a little strange, but she explained:

(MOLLY.) I never want tomorrow to come because no tomorrow will ever be as good as today.

She collected a handful of small pebbles from the shallows of the river.

(MOLLY.) I'm going to tell the future. I've seen the gypsies do it.

> (*She shakes the pebbles around in her cupped hands, closes her eyes and then scatters them out on to the muddy shore.*)

(MOLLY.) The stones say we'll always be together, the three of us, for ever and ever. They say that as long as we all stick together we'll all be lucky and happy. And the stones never lie. So you're stuck with me.

> (*Sound: summer buzz; animals and birds.*)

BROOK / MEADOW

Another time, Molly and Charlie and I were fishing down in the brook. It was late on a summer evening and we were just about to set off home when we heard the distant sound of an engine.

> (*Sound: intermittent droning, like a thousand stuttering bees.*)

At first we thought it was the Colonel's car – his Rolls-Royce was the only car for miles around – but it wasn't coming from the road at all; it was coming from somewhere high above us.

An aeroplane!

It circled above us like some ungainly yellow bird. We could see the goggled pilot looking down at us out of the cockpit. We waved up at him and he waved back. Then he seemed to be flying towards us, lower, lower.

It bounced, then bumped, then came to a stop just in front of us. The pilot beckoned us over.

(PILOT. *Shouting over the roar of the engine.*) Better not switch off! Might never get the damn thing started again. Listen, the truth is, I reckon I'm a bit lost. That church up there on the hill, is that Lapford church?

(CHARLIE. *Shouting back.*) No, that's Iddesleigh. St James's.

(PILOT. *Shouting.*) Iddesleigh? You sure?

(CHARLIE. *Shouting.*) Yes!

(PILOT. *Shouting.*) Whoops! Then I really was lost. Jolly good thing I stopped, wasn't it? Thanks for your help. Better be off. Here. Do you like humbugs?

And he handed us a bag of sweets.

(PILOT. *Shouting.*) Cheerio then. Stand well back. Here we go.

(*Sound: the plane splutters off.*)

He went bouncing along towards the hedge – and lifted off just in time, his wheels clipping the top, before he was up, up, and away. He did one steep turn, then flew straight at us. We threw ourselves face down in the long grass, feeling the blast of the wind as he flew over us. By the time we rolled over he was climbing up over the trees, over St James's church tower and away into the distance. And then he was gone.

(*Sound: just the buzzing summer silence again. A skylark sings.*)

For some time afterwards we lay there in the long grass watching a single skylark rising above us as we sucked on our humbugs.

(TOMMO.) Was that real, Charlie? Did it really happen?

(CHARLIE.) We've got our humbugs, Tommo, so it must have been real, mustn't it?

3

BARN

Ten to midnight.

I'm not sure I ever really believed in God, even in Sunday school. In church I'd gaze up at Jesus hanging on the cross in the stained-glass window, and feel sorry for him because I could see how cruel it was and how much it must be hurting him. I knew he was a good and kind man. But what I never really understood was why God, who was supposed to be his father, and almighty and powerful, would let them do that to him, would let him suffer so much. I believed then, as I believe now, that crossed fingers and Molly's stones are every bit as reliable or unreliable as praying to God. But if there's no God, does that mean there's no heaven? Tonight I want to believe there's a heaven; that there is a new life after death, like Father said, that death is not a full stop.

HOME

After my twelfth birthday, Charlie and Molly left school. I was alone, a big'un in Mr Munnings' class. I hated him now more than I feared him. Charlie and Molly found work up in the Big House: Molly as an under-parlour maid, and Charlie in the Colonel's hunt kennels.

Charlie would come home late in the cold evenings, hang up his coat on Father's peg and put his boots outside in the porch where Father's boots had always been and warm his feet in the bottom oven, just as Father had done. That was the first time in my life I was ever really jealous of Charlie. I wanted to warm my feet in the oven, to come home from proper work, to earn money like Charlie did. Most of all though I wanted Charlie and Molly and me to be together again, for everything to be just as it had been. (But nothing stays the same.)

When I did see Molly, and it was only on Sundays now, she was as kind to me as she'd always been, but too kind almost, more like a mother to me than a friend. Her hair was cut shorter now, the plaits were gone, and that changed the whole look of her. Molly wasn't a girl any more.

Then Charlie had a serious run-in with the Colonel and left his job up at the Big House and found work at Farmer Cox's on the other side of the village, so I saw even less of him than before. But we didn't see Molly at all any more. She'd suddenly stopped coming round – so Charlie sent me to her cottage with a letter.

OUTSIDE MOLLY'S COTTAGE

Molly's mother met me at the door:

(MOLLY'S MOTHER. *Her face like thunder.*) Go away. Just go away. We don't want you Peacefuls here. We don't want you bothering our Molly. And she doesn't want to see you. Go on!

I was walking away, Charlie's letter in my pocket, when I happened to glance back: Molly was waving at me frantically through her window, mouthing something I couldn't understand, pointing down the hill towards the brook.

BROOK

I ran down and waited. Molly soon arrived, hot and bothered:

(MOLLY.) The Colonel came to our cottage and told mother and father that he had dismissed Charlie because he had been seeing more of me than was good for me. They won't let me see Charlie any more. They won't let me see any of you. I'm so miserable without you, Tommo. I hate it up at the Big House, and I hate it at home too.

I leant over and kissed her on the cheek. She threw her arms around me, sobbing as if her heart would break.

(MOLLY.) I want to see Charlie. I miss him so much.

It was only then that I remembered to give her the letter. She tore it open and read it at once.

(MOLLY.) Tell him yes. Yes, I will.

That was the first of dozens of letters I delivered from Charlie to Molly and from Molly to Charlie over the weeks and months that followed. I was their go-between postman. Molly and I would meet most evenings and exchange letters in the same place, down by the brook. We'd sit and talk for a few precious minutes, often with the rain dripping through the trees. Once the wind roared so violently that I feared the trees might come down on us, so we ran out across the meadow and burrowed our way under a haystack and sat there shivering like a couple of frightened rabbits. It was in the shelter of this haystack that I first heard about the war.

It was Molly's job every morning to iron the Colonel's newspaper before she took it to him in his study – he insisted his *Times* should be crisp and dry, so that the ink would not come off on his fingers while he was reading it. I didn't really know about the war, but I learned that some archduke – whatever that was – had been shot in a place called Sarajevo – wherever that was – and Germany and France – I knew where they were – were very angry with each other about it. They were gathering their armies to fight each other and, if they did, then Great Britain would soon be in it too because we'd have to fight on the French side against the Germans.

In the meantime there were bigger bombshells closer to home.

HAY FIELD / HOME

Charlie and I had been haymaking with Farmer Cox – I was working with Charlie now; I'd finally left school and Mr Munnings far behind me. I'd thought about working for the Colonel: five generations of Peacefuls, six including Charlie, had done so before me; and it was tempting to work with

Molly. But I knew I wanted to work alongside Charlie more than anything else in the world – So, we were haymaking with Farmer Cox, buzzards wheeling above us all day long, swallows skimming the mown grass, as if Father was there watching over us. When we arrived home later than usual, dusty and hungry, Mother was sitting bolt upright in her chair doing her sewing and opposite her: Molly – a leather suitcase under the window sill.

(TOMMO.) What is it? What's up?

Molly didn't answer me. Mother spoke for her:

(MOTHER.) They've thrown her out. The Colonel, her mother and father have thrown her out, and it's your fault, Charlie.

Charlie looked confused:

(CHARLIE.) What's happened? What's going on?

Molly shook her head. Charlie looked at Mother. Mother looked at Charlie:

(MOTHER.) What's going on, Charlie, is that she's going to have your baby, that's what.

BEDROOM

That night I lay there in our room beside Charlie, not speaking. I was so filled with anger towards him that I never wanted to speak to him, nor Molly, ever again. Then Charlie spoke:

(CHARLIE.) It wasn't just letters, Tommo, you see… We didn't want to hide it from you, Tommo, honest. But we didn't want to hurt you either. Because you love her, don't you? Well, so do I, Tommo. I love her. Friends?

(*Pause.*)

(TOMMO.) Friends.

CHURCH

They were married up in the church a short time later, a very empty church. There was no one there except the vicar and the five of us, and the vicar's wife sitting at the back. Everyone knew about the baby by now, so the vicar only agreed to marry them on certain conditions: 'that no bells are rung, no hymns sung'. He rushed through the marriage service as if he wanted to be somewhere else. There was no wedding feast afterwards, only a cup of tea and a slice of fruit cake when we got home.

BIG JOE'S ROOM

I moved into Big Joe's room and slept with him in his bed, which wasn't easy because Big Joe was big, and the bed very narrow. He talked loudly to himself in his dreams, and tossed and turned all night long. But, as I lay awake, what troubled me more was that in the next room slept the two people I loved most in all the world who, in finding each other, had deserted me.

At home, I tried never to be alone with Molly – I didn't know what to say to her any more. I tried to avoid Charlie, too. On the farm, I took every opportunity that came my way to work on my own. Farmer Cox was always sending me off on some errand or other and I always took my time about it.

MARKET

It was while I was making a delivery to Hatherleigh market (one morning) that I came face to face with the war for the first time.

(*Sound: market noise; drums pounding, bugles blaring.*)

Behind the band there must have been a dozen soldiers, splendid in their scarlet uniforms. They marched past me, arms swinging in perfect time, polished buttons, boots shining, the sun glinting on their bayonets. Children were stomping alongside them, some in paper hats, some with wooden sticks over their shoulders. And there were women throwing flowers, roses mostly, their thorns hooking to the soldiers' tunics. Everyone followed.

(*Sound: band plays 'God Save the King'.*)

The Union Jack fluttering behind him, the first sergeant major I'd ever set eyes on got up on to the steps in the middle of the town square.

(SERGEANT MAJOR. *Commanding.*) Ladies and gentlemen, boys and girls! I shan't beat about the bush. I shan't tell you it's all tickety-boo out there in France – there's been too much of that nonsense already in my view. I've been there. I've seen it for myself. So I'll tell you straight. It's no picnic. It's an 'ard slog. But there's only one question to ask yourself about this war. Who would you rather see marching through your streets? Us lot, or the Hun? Because, mark my words, ladies and gentlemen, if we don't stop them out there in France, the Germans will be here, right here on your doorstep. They'll come marching through burning your houses, violating your women, killing your children. They've beaten brave little Belgium, swallowed her up in one gulp. And now they've taken a fair slice of France too. Unless we beat them at their own game, they'll gobble us up as well. Well? Do you want the Hun here? Do you?

'No!' came the shout, and I was shouting along with them.

(SERGEANT MAJOR.) Shall we beat the living daylights out of them then?

'Yes!' we roared.

(SERGEANT MAJOR.) Good. Then we shall need you. (*Pointing, like Kitchener, into the crowd.*) Your King needs you. Your country needs you. And all the brave lads out in France need you too. (*His face breaks into a smile.*) And remember one thing, lads – and I can vouch for this – all the ladies love a soldier.

The girls all laughed and giggled. The young men blushed.

(SERGEANT MAJOR.) So, who'll be the first brave lad to come and take the King's shilling? Who'll lead the way? I'm looking for boys with hearts of oak, lads who love their King and country, men what hates the lousy Hun.

Then the first one stepped forward. I recognised him at once: it was big Jimmy Parsons, the boy Charlie had hit in the goolies. Egged on by the cheering crowd, others soon followed.

Suddenly someone prods me hard in the small of my back – a toothless old lady is pointing at me with her crooked finger.

(TOOTHLESS OLD LADY. *Croaking.*) Go on, son, you go and fight. It's every man's duty to fight when his country calls, that's what I say. Go on. Y'ain't a coward, are you?

I didn't run, not at first. I sidled away from her slowly, backing out of the crowd hoping no one would notice me.

(TOOTHLESS OLD LADY.) Chicken! Chicken!

Then I ran helter-skelter from the crowded square, down the deserted High Street.

(TOOTHLESS OLD LADY.) Chicken!

Filled with shame, I keep on going, the Toothless Old Lady's words ringing in my ears, thinking about what the Sergeant Major has said, about how fine and manly the men looked, how Molly would admire me in my scarlet uniform, maybe even love me if I joined up. I ran all the way home.

KITCHEN

We'd barely sat down for supper before I began:

(TOMMO.) Farmer Cox sent me to market this morning. The army was there, recruiting. Jimmy Parsons joined up. Lots of others too.

Then Mother interrupted me:

(MOTHER.) Don't worry about it, Tommo, they can't make you go. You're too young anyway.

(TOMMO.) I'm nearly sixteen.

(CHARLIE.) You've got to be nineteen to serve overseas, Tommo, they don't want boys.

(I guessed Charlie was right.) Then Molly joined in, her hand resting on her pregnant belly:

(MOLLY.) They shouldn't take the men either. What are the women supposed to do, fend for themselves? What about the mothers? You wouldn't go Charlie, would you?

(CHARLIE.) I'll be honest, Moll. It's been bothering me a lot just lately. I don't want to go. I'd shoot a rat because it might bite me. I'd shoot a rabbit because I can eat it. Why would I ever want to shoot a German? Never even met a German. But I've seen the lists in the papers – y'know, all the killed and the wounded. Pages of them. Poor beggars. It hardly seems right, does it: me being here, enjoying life, while they're over there. (It's not all bad, Moll.) I saw Benny Copplestone yesterday, sporting his uniform up at the pub. He's back on leave. He says we've got the Germans on the run now. One big push, he reckons, and we'll have 'em running back to Berlin with their tails between their legs, and then all our boys can come home. With a bit of luck I'll be back to wet the baby's head. And Tommo will look after you. He'll be the man about the place, won't you, Tommo?

(TOMMO.) I'm not staying, Charlie. I'm coming with you.

I loved what I knew: and what I knew was my family, and Molly, and the countryside I'd grown up in. I would do all I could to protect the people I loved. And I would do it with Charlie.

(Optional Interval.)

4

BARN

A quarter past two.

I'm not sleepy.

I should be able to fight off sleep by now. I've done it often enough on look-out in the trenches. I used to long for that moment when you surrender to sleep, when you drift away into the warmth of nothingness. After this night is over, I can drift away, I can sleep for ever.

(*Sound: steam train.*)

TRAIN

On the train to Exeter, Charlie gave me my instructions:

(CHARLIE.) You'll have to behave like a nineteen year old from now on, Tommo. You follow my lead.

REGIMENTAL DEPOT

When the time came, in front of the Recruiting Officer at the regimental depot, I stood as tall as I could and let Charlie speak for us both.

(CHARLIE.) I'm Charlie Peaceful, and he's Thomas Peaceful. We're twins and we're volunteering.

(RECRUITING OFFICER.) Date of birth?

(CHARLIE.) 5th of October, '95.

(RECRUITING OFFICER.) Both of you?

(CHARLIE.) Course, only I'm older than him by one hour. And that was that. Easy. We were in.

TRAINING GROUND

(SERGEANT HANLEY.) Stand still! Stomach in, chest out! Look to your front, Peaceful, you horrible little man! Down in that mud, Peaceful, where you belong, you nasty little worm!

Sergeant Horrible Hanley. Our chief tormentor at training camp on Salisbury Plain. He would do his utmost to make all our lives a misery. And one life in particular: Charlie's.

(SERGEANT HANLEY.) Are you the best they can send us these days, Peaceful? Vermin, that's what you are. Lousy vermin, and I've got to make a soldier out of you. What's with this cap badge, Peaceful? It's crooked. You are a blot on creation, Peaceful. What are you?

(CHARLIE. *Clear, firm, utterly without fear.*) Happy to be here, Sergeant.

The boots they gave us were far too big – they hadn't got any smaller sizes. So we clomped about like clowns – clowns in tin hats and khaki.

There were dozens of others under-age in the regiment – they needed all the young men they could get. Sometimes the older lads teased me about being so young, but Charlie would give them a little look and they'd soon stop. Then Sergeant Hanley began picking on me.

We'd been drilling one morning, and were stood to attention, when Hanley grabbed my rifle:

(SERGEANT HANLEY. *Looking down the barrel.*) Dirty.

We all knew the punishment: five times at the double around the parade ground, holding your rifle above your head. After only two circuits I just couldn't keep my rifle up.

(SERGEANT HANLEY. *Bellowing.*) Every time you let that rifle fall, Peaceful, you begin the punishment again! Five more, Peaceful.

My head is swimming. My back's on fire. I'm staggering. I hear a shout:

Charlie has broken ranks and he runs at Hanley, screaming, telling him exactly what he thinks of him.

For that, Charlie was tied to a gun wheel. 'Field Punishment Number One', the Brigadier called it:

(BRIGADIER.) Private Peaceful has got off lightly. Insubordination in a time of war could be seen as mutiny, and mutiny is punishable by death, by firing squad.

As we march past him, Charlie smiles at me. I try to smile back, but no smile came. To me, Charlie looks like Jesus hanging on the cross at St James's church back home in Iddesleigh.

5

BARN

A minute past three.

I keep checking the time. Each time I do it, I put the watch to my ear and listen for the tick. It's still there, softly slicing away the seconds, then the minutes, then the hours. Charlie told me this watch would never stop, never let me down, unless I forgot to wind it. The best watch in the world, he said, a wonderful watch. But if it was such a wonderful watch it would do more than simply keep time – any old watch can do that. A truly wonderful watch would make time. Then, if it stopped, time itself would have to stand still, then this night would never have to end and morning would never come.

Charlie always said we were living on borrowed time out here.

(*Sings.*) Oranges and Lemons, say the bells of St Clement's,

You owe me five farthings, say the bells of St Martin's.
When will you pay me? say the bells of Old Bailey.
When I grow rich, say the bells of Shoreditch.
When will that be? say the bells of Stepney.
I'm sure I don't know, says the great bell of Bow.
Here comes a candle to light you to bed,
And here comes a chopper to chop off your head.
Chip, Chop, Chip, Chop, the last – man's –

They tell us we're going over to France, and we're all relieved. We're leaving Sergeant Hanley far behind us.

(*Sound: ship's horn.*)

QUAYSIDE

When our ship docks in Boulogne, every voice I hear from the quayside below us…is English, every uniform and every helmet like our own. Then, as we come down the gangplank into the fresh morning air, we see them close to: the walking wounded shuffling along the quayside towards us, some with their eyes bandaged, holding on to the shoulder of the one in front. Others lie on stretchers. One of them, puffing on a cigarette looks at me out of sunken yellow eyes:

(SOLDIER.) G'luck lads. Give 'em what for.

MARCHING TO THE FRONT

We don't stay long in France but march into Belgium.

(*Sound: two aeroplanes buzzing overhead.*)

Two aeroplanes are chasing each other in the distance. They are too far away for us to see which of them is ours. We make up our minds it's the smaller one and cheer for him madly, and I'm wondering if the pilot from the yellow plane might be up there. I can almost taste the humbugs he gave us as I watch them. I lose them in the sun – and then the smaller one spirals earthwards and our cheering instantly stops.

(*Sound: estaminet hubbub.*)

ESTAMINET

After arriving at rest camp, they let us out for an evening
to go into the nearest village, to an estaminet, a sort of pub,
where there's the best beer and best egg and chips in the entire
world. We stuff ourselves.

There's a girl there who smiles at me when she clears the
plates away. She's the daughter of the owner. He is very
smartly dressed and very round and very merry, like a Father
Christmas but without the beard. It's difficult to believe
she's his daughter – she's the opposite in every way: elf-like,
delicate. Charlie and me drink ourselves silly – I'm properly
drunk for the first time in my life and feel very proud of
myself. We stagger back to camp and flop off to sleep.

FRONT LINE

The next day we march towards the line – it seems as if the
road is taking us down into the earth itself, until it is a road no
more but a tunnel without a roof, a communications trench.
We have to be silent now. Not a whisper, not a word. If the
German machine-gunners spot us, we're done for. A line of
soldiers passes us coming the other way, dark-eyed men. No
need for questions. No need for answers…

We find our dug-out at last. *(He turns the bed on its side to make
the dug-out and trench.)* It has been a long, cold march. All
I want is a mug of hot sweet tea and a lie down – but with
Charlie, I'm posted on sentry duty.

TRENCH

For the first time I look out through the wire into no-man's-
land and towards the enemy trenches. Less than two hundred
yards from our front line, they tell us. There's no smoking in
the trenches at night – not unless we want our heads shot off

by snipers spotting the red glow of the cigarette tip. The night is still now.

(CHARLIE. *Whispering.*) It's a fine night for poaching, Tommo.

(*Sound: artillery.*)

Suddenly, our artillery lobs a shell over into their trenches, and they do the same back. This terrifies me. Then it happens again and in time I get used to it.

Our trench and our dug-outs have been left a right mess by the previous soldiers and we clear it all up, because of the rats. Rats. I'm the first one to find them. I am detailed to shore up a dilapidated trench wall. I plunge my shovel in and open up an entire nest of them. They come pouring out, skittering away over my boots. For a moment I'm horrified – but then I set about stamping them to death in the mud. I don't kill a single one.

Our other daily curse is lice. Each of us has to burn off his own with a lighted cigarette end. They nestle in wherever they can: the folds of your skin, the creases of your clothes. We long for a bath to drown the lot of them.

(*Sound: rain.*)

Our greatest scourge is neither rats nor lice but the unending rain. It runs like a stream along the bottom of our trench, turning it into a mud-filled ditch, a stinking gooey mud that seems to want to hold you and then suck you down and drown you.

It's Charlie who keeps us all together. He's like a big brother to everyone. Being his real brother, I could feel I live in his shadow but I don't, I live in his glow.

Word has come down from headquarters that we must send out patrols to find out what regiments have come into the line opposite us. Why we have to do this we do not know – there are spotter planes doing it almost every day. My turn soon comes up. Charlie's too. Captain Wilkie's heading the patrol and he tells us –

(CAPTAIN WILKIE.) 'We have to bring back a prisoner for questioning'.

They give us a double rum ration, and I'm warmed instantly to the roots of my hair, to my very toenails.

On the signal, we climb up over the top and crawl on our bellies through the wire.

NO-MAN'S-LAND

We snake our way forward. It takes an eternity to cross no-man's-land. I'm beginning to wonder if we'll ever find their trenches at all. We slither into a shell hole and lie doggo there for a while. We can hear Fritz talking now, and laughing – and playing music.

(*Sound: a distant gramophone plays.*)

We're close now, very close. I'm not scared – I'm excited. I'm out poaching with Charlie. I'm tensed for danger.

Then we see the wire up ahead. We wriggle through a gap and drop down into their trench.

GERMAN TRENCH

It looks deserted, but we can still hear the voices and the music. I notice their trench is much deeper than ours, wider too and more solidly constructed. I grip my rifle tight and follow Charlie along the trench, bent double like everyone else.

(TOMMO.) We're making too much noise. I can't understand why no one has heard us. Where are their sentries, for God's sake?

At that moment, a German soldier comes out of a dug-out. For a split second the Hun does nothing and neither do we. We just stand and look at one another. Then he lets out a shriek, and blunders back into the dug-out. I don't know who threw the grenade in after him, (*Sound: blast.*) but there is a blast that throws me back against the trench wall. There is screaming and firing from inside the dug-out. Then silence. The music has stopped. We peer in through the smoke. Several German soldiers are lying sprawled out, all dead – except one. He stands there naked, blood-spattered, shaking. I'm shaking. He has his hands in the air and is whimpering. Captain Wilkie throws a coat over him and bundles him out. We scrabble our way up over the top of the German trench, through the wire – and run.

NO-MAN'S-LAND

For a while I think we have got away with it – but then a flare goes up and we are caught suddenly in broad daylight. I hurl myself to the ground.

(*Sound: machine-gun rattle, rifles popping.*)

There is nowhere to hide, so we pretend to be dead. Eyes closed, I'm thinking of Molly. If I'm going to die I want my last thought to be of her. But instead I'm saying sorry to Father for what I did, that I didn't mean to kill him.

We wait till the light dies and the night is suddenly black again. Captain Wilkie gets us to our feet and we go on, running, stumbling. Then the shelling starts. We dive into a crater.

(*Sound: shelling.*)

It seems as if we have woken up the entire German army. I cower with the German and Charlie, the three of us clinging together.

(GERMAN SOLDIER.) Lieber Gott! Lieber Gott!

'Gott.' They call God by the same name. He's praying.

Then we see the Captain lying higher up the slope; Charlie goes up and turns him over:

(CAPTAIN WILKIE.) I won't make it. I'm leaving it to you to get them all back, Peaceful, and the prisoner. Go on now.

(CHARLIE.) No, sir. If one goes, we all go. Isn't that right, lads?

Under the cover of an early-morning mist we make it back to our trenches, Charlie carrying the Captain on his back the whole way until the stretcher bearers came for him. As they lifted him up, Captain Wilkie held Charlie by the hand:

(CAPTAIN WILKIE.) Take my watch, Peaceful. You've given me more time on this earth.

(CHARLIE. *Admiring the watch*.) It's wonderful, sir. Ruddy wonderful.

FRONT LINE

The next time they send us up the line it is into the Wipers' salient itself, where our own lines had encroached into the enemy territory. Everyone knew Fritz had us surrounded and overlooked on three sides – they could chuck all they wanted into our trenches and all we could do was grin and bear it. We had a new company commander, Lieutenant Buckland. He told us how things were:

(LIEUTENANT BUCKLAND.) If we give way then Wipers will be lost. Wipers must not be lost.

He didn't say why it mustn't be lost but he was doing his best. He was straight out from England, very properly spoken, but he knew even less about fighting this war than we did. He seemed younger than any of us, even me.

WIPERS

As we march through Wipers I wonder why it is worth fighting for at all. There was no town left; nothing you could call a town anyway. Rubble and ruin, more dogs and cats than civilians. None of us sang. None of us talked.

TRENCHES

When we get to the new trenches, there is a sickly-sweet stench about the place that has to be more than stagnant mud and water. We all knew well enough what it was, but we don't speak about it.

I'm on stand-to the next morning.

The mist rises over no-man's-land.

I see in front of me a blasted wasteland.

No fields or trees,

not a blade of grass –

simply a land of mud and craters.

I see unnatural humps

scattered over there beyond our wire:

the unburied,

some in field-grey uniforms and some in khaki.

There's a German soldier lying in the wire

with his arm stretched heavenwards,

his hand pointing.

There are birds up there,

and they are singing.

We're back down in the dug-out after stand-to, brewing up when the bombardment starts.

(*Sound: bombardment.*)

It doesn't stop for two whole days. They are the longest two days of my life. We can not talk. We can not think. When I do manage to sleep I see the hand pointing skywards, and it is Father's hand, and I wake shaking. I cry like a baby and not even Charlie can comfort me. We want it to stop, even though we know that when it's over they'll be coming for us with the gas maybe, or the flame-thrower, or the grenades, or the bayonets. Let them come. I just want this to stop. I want it to be over.

When at last it does stop we are ordered out on to the firestep, bayonets fixed, eyes straining through the smoke that drifts across in front of us.

(*Sound: music – Holst's 'Mars' from* The Planets.)

Then out of the smoke we see them come, their bayonets glinting, one or two at first, but then hundreds, thousands.

The firing starts all along the line – and I'm firing too, not aiming, just firing. Firing. Firing. Loading my rifle and firing. And still the Germans do not stop. They come towards us, an invincible army. I can see their wild eyes as they reach our wire. It's the wire that stops them, and those that find the gaps are shot down before they ever reach our trenches. The others have turned now and are stumbling back. I feel a surge of triumph welling inside me, not because we have won, but because I have stood with the others. I have not run.

(TOOTHLESS OLD LADY.) Y'ain't a coward, are you?

No, old woman, I am not.

Then the cry goes up:

'Gas! Gas! Gas!'

(*Sound: bell.*)

It is echoed all along the line. For a moment we are frozen in terror. We see it rolling towards us, this dreaded killer cloud we have heard so much about. Its deadly tendrils are searching ahead, feeling their way forward in long yellow wisps, scenting me, searching for me. Then seeing me, the gas turns and drifts straight for me:

(TOMMO.) Christ! Christ!

I tell myself I will not breathe. I see men running, staggering, falling. I have to breathe now. I can't run without breathing. Half-blinded by the gas mask I trip and fall. My gas mask has come off. I pull it back on, but I have breathed in and already my eyes are stinging, my lungs are burning. I am coughing, retching, choking. I don't care where I'm running so long as it's away from the gas – and then I'm out of it.

(*TOMMO wrenches off his mask, gasping for good air.*)

I look up through blurred and weeping eyes. A Hun in his own gas mask is standing over me, his rifle pointing at my head.

(*TOMMO braces himself.*)

(GERMAN SOLDIER.) Go boy! Go, Tommy, go!

So by the whim of some kind and unknown Fritz I survive and escape.

FIELD HOSPITAL

Later, at the field hospital, I hear that we counter-attacked, retaking our front-line trenches; but, from what I could see all around me, it was at a terrible cost. All that attack and all that death, for nothing. No gains on either side. I line up with the rest of the walking wounded to see the doctor. He washes out my eyes, examines them, and listens to my chest.

(DOCTOR.) You were lucky. You can only have caught a whiff of it.

As I walk away I pass the others who have not been so lucky, rows of them, lying stretched out in the sun, many of them faces I knew, and would never see again: corpses.

ESTAMINET

That evening I was in the estaminet drowning my anger in beer. And it was anger I was drowning, not sorrows. In my befuddled state I even thought of deserting: I'd make my way to the English Channel and find a boat. I'd get home somehow.

I look around me. There must have been a hundred or more soldiers in the place that evening but they all looked as alone as I felt. It's stiflingly hot in there and the air is thick with cigarette smoke – like the gas. I can hardly breathe. It gives me the shakes. I went outside to get some air.

(ANNA.) Tommy?

It was her. She was carrying out a crate of wine bottles.

(ANNA.) You are ill?

We stood for some moments. I want to speak, but I don't trust myself. I felt suddenly overwhelmed by tears, by a longing for home and for Molly.

(ANNA.) How old?

(TOMMO.) Sixteen.

(ANNA.) Like me. I have seen you before I think?

(*TOMMO nods.*)

(ANNA.) My name is Anna.

(TOMMO.) My name is Tommo.

(ANNA.) It's true then, every English soldier is called Tommy.

(TOMMO.) No, not Tommy; I'm Tommo.

STABLE

I told her I worked on a farm and she took me into the stable and showed me her father's carthorse. He was massive and magnificent. Our hands met as we patted him. She kissed me then, brushed my cheek with her lips.

ROAD

I left her and walked back to camp under the high-riding moon, singing at the top of my voice:

(TOMMO. *Singing*.) Oranges and Lemons say the bells of St Clement's…

CAMP

Charlie greeted me at the camp with a smirk:

(CHARLIE.) You won't be so ruddy happy, Tommo, not when you hear what I've got to tell you. Our new sergeant. It's only Horrible-Bleeding-Hanley.

6

BARN

Nearly four o'clock.

There is the beginning of day in the sky, not the pale light of dawn yet, but night is certainly losing its darkness.

CAMP

We get plenty of letters at rest camp – they come far swifter to the front than they do at home. Charlie has been fretting about Molly and has written to her every day. Then one morning, we both receive a letter in Molly's handwriting. Charlie opens his – and weeps. I open mine –

(MOLLY.) My dear Tommo,

> I write to say that I have had a darling boy. Charlie and I agreed on his name before you both went away: Tommo, after his brave uncle. One day, when this dreadful war is over, we shall be together again and young Tommo will see his father and his uncle for the first time and smile. Big Joe already smiles at him. And little Tommo has Big Joe's great grin – and Charlie's (black) hair, and your (hazel) eyes. Because of all this I love him more than I can say.
>
> Your Molly.

I caught sight of Charlie. He was wiping away his tears. He was looking more determined than ever – and I could see why.

(CHARLIE.) Sergeant Hanley, what a nice surprise. I heard you'd joined us.

(SERGEANT HANLEY.) I'm warning you, Peaceful, I've got my eye on you. One step out of line…

(CHARLIE.) Don't worry about me, Sergeant. I'll be as good as gold. Cross my heart and hope to die.

ROAD

Once again we find ourselves marching up into the trenches, along with hundreds of others, 'to stiffen the line' they told us, which could only mean one thing: a big attack was expected and we would be in for a packet of trouble.

(*Sound: shell whine.*)

TRENCH

The blast throws us all to the ground, it is the first shell of thousands. Our big guns answer almost at once, and the world above us erupts.

(*Sound: bombardment.*)

Every heavy gun the Germans have seems to be aimed at our sector. It's terrifying. I find myself curled into a ball on the ground and screaming for it to stop. Then I feel Charlie lying beside me, folding himself around me to protect me.

(CHARLIE. *Singing.*) Oranges and Lemons say the bells of St Clement's…

– and soon I am singing with him, singing instead of screaming. 'You owe me five farthings…' (*Etc.*) And before we know it the whole dug-out is singing along with us. But the barrage goes on and on and on, until in the end neither Charlie nor 'Oranges and Lemons' can drive away the terror that is engulfing me, invading me, destroying any last glimmer of courage I have left. All I have now is my fear.

When the German attack comes, it falters before it ever reaches our wire. When they turn and run, we wait for the whistle and then go out over the top.

(*Sound: whistle.*)

NO-MAN'S-LAND

I go because the others go, moving forward as if in a trance, as if outside myself altogether. *(Sound: boom!)* There is blood pouring down my face, and my head is burning, such a terrible pain, and I feel myself falling, and it's warm and comforting and so quiet…

7

BARN

Twenty-five to six.

Twenty-five minutes to go. How shall I live them? Should I eat a hearty breakfast? I don't want it. Shall I scream and shout? What would be the point? Shall I pray? Why? What for? Who to?

No. They will do what they will do. General Haig has signed and he is God out here. Haig has confirmed the sentence. He has confirmed that 'Private Peaceful will die, will be shot for cowardice in the face of the enemy at six o'clock on the morning of the 25th of June 1916.'

They say there's soon going to be an almighty push all the way to Berlin. I've heard that before. They say the regiment is marching up the road towards the Somme. It is late June, summer here and at home, the Somme here for our troops, and…

The firing squad will be having their breakfast by now, sipping their tea.

No one has told me exactly where it will happen. I don't want it to be in some dark yard with grey walls all around. I want it to be where there is sky and clouds and trees, and birds.

(*Sound: muffled ordinance.*)

CONCRETE DUG-OUT

I wake to the muffled sound of machine-gun fire, to the distant blast of the shells. The earth quivers and trembles about me. It must be night and I am lying wounded somewhere in no-man's-land, looking up into the black of the sky. But then I try to move my head a little and the blackness begins to crumble and fall in on me, filling my mouth, my eyes, my ears. It is not the sky I am looking at, but earth. I am buried, buried alive – they must have thought I was dead and buried me. But I am not dead. I'm not! My fingers scrabble, clawing frantically at the earth – and then I feel something. Another body. And I hear a voice:

(CHARLIE.) Thought we'd lost you, Tommo. The same shell that buried you killed half a dozen of the others. You were lucky. Your head looks a bit of a mess, though. Me, I can't feel my legs. I think I've lost a lot of blood.

(TOMMO.) Where are we, Charlie?

(CHARLIE.) Middle of bloody no-man's-land, that's where, some old German dug-out.

(TOMMO.) We'd best stay put for a while, hadn't we, Charlie?

(SERGEANT HANLEY.) Stay put? Stay put? You're worse than your brother, Peaceful. Our orders are to press home the attack and then hold our ground. Only fifty yards or so to the German trenches. On your feet, all of you.

(*No one moves.*)

(SERGEANT HANLEY.) What in hell's name is the matter with you lot? On your feet, damn you! On your feet!

Then I hear myself speaking, quietly at first:

(TOMMO.) I think we're all thinking the same thing, Sergeant. You take us out there now and the German machine-guns will mow us down. Maybe we should stay here and then go back later when it gets dark? No point in going out there and getting ourselves killed for nothing, is there Sergeant?

(SERGEANT HANLEY.) Are you disobeying my order, Private Peaceful?

(TOMMO.) No, I'm just letting you know what I think. What we all think.

(SERGEANT HANLEY.) And I'm telling you, Peaceful, that if you don't come with us when we go, it won't be field punishment like your brother got, it'll be a court martial. It'll be the firing squad. Do you hear me, Peaceful? Do you hear me?

(TOMMO.) Yes, Sergeant. I hear you. But the thing is, Sergeant, even if I wanted to, I can't go with you because I'd have to leave Charlie behind, and I can't do that. He's wounded. I don't think he can walk, let alone run. I'm not leaving him.

(SERGEANT HANLEY.) You miserable little worm, Peaceful. I should shoot you right where you are and save the firing squad the trouble. The rest of you, on your feet. I want you men out there. It's a court martial for anyone who stays.

One by one the men get unwillingly to their feet, each one preparing himself in his own way, a last smoke on a shielded cigarette, a silent prayer.

(SERGEANT HANLEY. *Screaming.*) Let's go! Let's go!

(*Sound: the German machine-guns open fire.*)

(TOMMO.) Poor beggars.

Then Charlie speaks:

(CHARLIE.) I'm not sure I'm going to make it, Tommo. I want you to have this.

(*CHARLIE takes off his watch.*)

(CHARLIE.) It's a wonderful watch, this. It will never let you down. If you wind it regular, time will never stop and when you get back home, little Tommo can have it. He's got all the time in the world.

Then Charlie spoke no more. And I must have slept, because when I open my eyes, there is Sergeant Hanley staring at me from under his helmet, cold hate in his eyes.

We waited, but by nightfall there was no sign of the others who had joined the Sergeant on that futile charge.

NO-MAN'S-LAND

In the dark of the night, we stumble back to our trench across no-man's-land, me carrying Charlie, giving him a piggyback all the way.

BARN

It wasn't a proper trial. They'd made up their minds I was guilty before they even sat down. I had three of them: a brigadier and two captains. I told them everything. I wasn't going to hide anything:

(TOMMO.) Yes, I did disobey Sergeant Hanley's order. The order was stupid, suicidal – we all knew it was – and I had to stay behind to look after my brother, Charlie.

They knew a dozen or more got wiped out in that attack. They knew I was right, but it made no difference. Because there's a big push coming, they want to make an example of someone.

The brigadier said I was a worthless man. Worthless.

Molly didn't think I was worthless. Charlie didn't think so either. Nor Mother, Big Joe, Father.

The whole court martial took less than an hour. That's all they gave me. One hour for a man's life.

Sound: a distant church bell chimes six o'clock.

TOMMO slowly leaves the stage.

Sound: a volley of shots.

Sound: music.

The End.

OTHER ADAPTATIONS BY SIMON READE

Pride and Prejudice
Jane Austen
9781840029512

The Scarecrow and His Servant
Philip Pullman
9781840028997

Not the End of the World
Geraldine McCaughrean
9781840027365

Private Peaceful & Other Plays
(Private Peaceful / Aladdin and the Enchanted Lamp /
The Owl Who Was Afraid of the Dark)
Michael Morpurgo, Philip Pullman, Jill Tomlinson
9781840026603

Twist Of Gold
Michael Morpurgo
9781849432061

OTHER TITLES BY SIMON READE

Dear Mr Shakespeare:
Letters to a Jobbing Playwright
9781840028294

WWW.OBERONBOOKS.COM

Follow us on www.twitter.com/@oberonbooks
& www.facebook.com/oberonbook